GRAHAM WHILEY & JANE CAVEN

Employment Law is not for the convenience of employers

Real, and often amusing, stories from leaders learning to live with their people

Copyright © 2019 by Graham Whiley & Jane Caven

All rights reserved. No part of this publication may be reproduced, stored or transmitted in any form or by any means, electronic, mechanical, photocopying, recording, scanning, or otherwise without written permission from the publisher. It is illegal to copy this book, post it to a website, or distribute it by any other means without permission.

Disclaimer: This book's aim is to share some of the situations we've witnessed in our professional lives. It is not intended as a comprehensive guide to HR or Employment Law, nor is it a replacement for legal or other expert advice. While every effort has been made to ensure the information within this book is accurate and up to date, mistakes or inaccuracies may exist. The authors accept no liability or responsibility for any loss or damage caused, or thought to be caused, by following the advice in this book and recommend you use it in conjunction with other trusted sources and information.

Illustrations © Clive Goddard 2019 www.clivegoddard.com

First edition

ISBN: 978-1-9161969-0-2

*This book was professionally typeset on Reedsy.
Find out more at reedsy.com*

Contents

Foreword	iv
Preface	vii
Don't	1
Don't discriminate	1
Don't harass	10
Don't underpay	35
Don't avoid the paperwork	40
Do	48
Do play fair	48
Do remember who's the boss	53
Do listen and watch	59
Remember	66
Remember: TUPE is tricky	66
Remember: redundancy is about roles not people	73
Remember: employees have responsibilities too	78
Remember: employment law has a few very sensitive areas	82
Remember: people management is constantly evolving	84
Epilogue	90

Foreword

People. That one commodity no organisation exists without.

If you are responsible for managing people in the workplace this book is for you. Dedicated to you, in fact. Because, although managing people is often rewarding, exhilarating and fun, it can also be a huge challenge and employment law can be very difficult to grapple with.

We share your pain.

This book is **not** a 'how to'. It's a window into our experience at the coalface; experience with *real* people, in *real* businesses, who need to get stuff done. We've boiled down our combined insights into what *really* works in the people management space and how to notice potential problems before they spiral out of control.

If that sounds like what you need then this book is for you. Enjoy.

With over 40 years' experience, co-author Jane Caven has run the successful Sagegreen HR advisory business since 2002. With seven offices around the country, a client base covering everything from global brands to SME's, public sector organisations to the rather vaguely named third sector, she and her team have pretty much seen it all.

They advise on everything from recruitment to employment law compliance, to organisational development – you know, the big strategic stuff – talent management, employee engagement, employer branding and cultural change. Jane even makes time to work as a qualified executive coach and mentor.

Before that she had a 'proper job' in corporate life. She held some of the biggest HR director roles in the country, with organisations like Glanbia, Booker and Adidas, and was responsible for thousands of employees across myriad locations and business sectors.

Jane knows her stuff. That stuff is the quite skillful blending of employment law and parallel regulations, with practical, business-focused, real-world application. If you have a people problem she'll know how to fix it. Not only that, she can navigate the legal framework to achieve a sensible outcome.

Graham Whiley also has more than 40 years' experience, having flown up the ranks from financial director at 25, to managing director at 32 and then CEO at 37. He started the Sagegreen HR business from scratch in 2000, which he has run in partnership with Jane since 2002. He combines that with three non-executive director roles. Along the way he has been involved in a number of mergers and acquisitions projects.

Graham, has worked with organisations of all sizes, across many sectors, both in the UK and globally. Sagegreen is an owner-managed SME and, as you might expect, also an employer. It was created from nothing and is completely self-funded with no debt.

Despite this hard-won experience and expertise in people management we have never written a book before. We've had advice and support along the way and we'd like to thank everyone who's been involved but essentially, we are author virgins. So please be gentle with us.

Jane and Graham - December 2019

(as an equal opportunities employer I was happy to be second - Graham)

Preface

'Employment Law is *NOT* for the convenience of employers.'

If you think that sounds like a legal professional might have said it, you'd be right. We heard it first in early corporate life when we were involved in preparing for an employment tribunal. The barrister needed to get our feet firmly rooted in the things that mattered to the members of the panel and not the ones that mattered to us (commercially).

If you have ever been involved, as a manager, in an employment tribunal then you will know they create high levels of emotion. As the employer you can often feel that you are guilty until proven innocent. It's not true, but it can feel like it, which can make the situation very stressful.

The reality is that employment law genuinely aims to reflect the values and norms that our society believes we should exhibit in our lives, generally, and in work specifically.

It can be a force for good. However, like all man-made law it can be imperfect, create unintended consequences and sometimes feel completely counter-intuitive.

So, yep, it can be an ass.

But remember, it doesn't mean to – honest.

As society's values keep evolving so does the law. Or put more prosaically, that's why there's a never ending stream of new regulations. I know it's fashionable to blame the EU for this but frankly we, the UK, have been pretty willing participants in the ongoing expansion of red tape in this area. Where our government felt the EU had gone too far they took the trouble to negotiate exemptions such as those around the 'working time directive' allowing employees to opt out of the 48-hour cap on the working week.

But, largely, the regulation we have today reflects what we want our world to look like and is a huge improvement on what we had in the past. Growing up in the 1960s and 70s, the world of work then - that is management techniques, acceptable behaviours and ways of talking to and treating people - would be unrecognisable today.

Here are some examples of what was acceptable then - when the power was most certainly in the hands of the employer:

- 'Stress is for wimps.'
- 'I employ you, not your family.'
- 'That's not a job for a girl!'
- 'You're not paid to think.'
- Demarcation (*if you can remember this you are older than you think! It was where roles were so well-defined and discrete that doing somebody else's job was deemed by unions as threatening jobs. Hard to imagine in our modern world, but true*)
- 'It's work. If it was meant to be fun it would be spelt F.U.N. not W.O.R.K.'
- 'Be the first in to the office and the last out.'
- 'You climb the greasy pole from the bottom up.'
- 'Men are the breadwinners. Women are the homemakers.'

- 'Experience comes with age.' *(implicitly saying young people should know their place and would not be promoted over older employees)*
- 'It's not what you know, it's who you know.'
- 'You're fired!' *(when the power to instantly dismiss was a reality)*
- 'Get your cards!' *(this expression was another version of 'you're fired', relating to formal National Insurance Cards and stamps that employees had to carry with them at work)*

Nowadays, causing offence to staff could easily lead to a formal complaint which could stigmatise a manager as sexist, racist, ageist, homophobic, misogynistic - at the very least.... or worst of all 'lacking emotional intelligence'.

All career limiting and even job threatening. So, who'd be a manager eh?

In this book, we are going to interpret the intentions of employment law in terms of what it wants to encourage or discourage. We are also going to highlight some not so obvious areas where managing people can be unexpectedly tricky. In particular, where the law may well defy common sense if not gravity.

All of this will be wrapped up in anecdotes; war stories if you will, from our hard-won experience. We may have to change some names to protect the innocent, and the not so innocent too!

There are three parts:

Part One
    DON'T! A review of the really important things employers must guard *against.*

Part Two

DO! A focus on areas where it pays for managers to be proactive.

Part Three

REMEMBER! As we will explain, a lot of employment regulation is not intuitive, so we will highlight some of those situations where it's a really good idea to keep your wits about you.

Let's crack on.

Don't

This is a review of the key things you *shouldn't do* as an employer or manager when dealing with your employees. It covers four important areas to guard against:
- Don't discriminate
- Don't harass
- Don't underpay
- Don't avoid the paperwork

Don't discriminate

Our society is increasingly on the side of the underdog. We genuinely want to see level playing fields in all aspects of life. We do not like to see people excluded, harmed or generally treated badly because they are 'not normal'. By 'normal' you might mean a number of things, but it might be summed up as being 'not like me' – where 'me' is the person or people making the decision.

However, we are still on a journey of defining discrimination as a society. That means there are inconsistencies and uncertainties that can look like double standards or reverse discrimination i.e. one person or group should not suffer discrimination but it is OK for that person or group to discriminate. Mariella Frostrup pointed out a relatively recent one. Quite understandably, we are all very sensitive to women being sexualised but there wasn't the same level of outrage when newspapers put a bare-chested Poldark on their front pages.

We will work this out in time and decide what is acceptable and what's not. In the meantime, this can leave managers and employers in a real quandary about what is a legally-compliant basis for a decision and what's not.

In simple terms, UK legislation says employers must not allow the following things to be relevant in any decision concerning an employee or potential employee:

- Age
- Gender
- Sexuality
- Ethnicity – colour, race, nationality
- Religion (or lack of)
- Disability (physical, mental, or serious illness)
- Pregnancy (usually only applies to females)
- Being in a trade union

Actually, it goes further. It holds the employer responsible for any situation arising around the work place where an employee feels they have suffered discrimination.

You know all of this.

But do you? Here's an example to test your reactions.

DON'T

Competing interpretations of discrimination

Our client runs a call centre. Let's call them Appointments R Us. Like a lot of these places it's full of relatively young people and it's very results driven. There's highly visible performance measuring and generally a bit of a boiler room atmosphere. There's nowhere to hide, it's a very mixed group of sexes and sexualities with a lot of high-energy personalities and large egos.

A male employee, a self-declared homosexual, started to refer to himself in the female third person when talking to other team members. He was saying things like 'she is not feeling so good today' and 'she had a fabulous evening'.

The women in the office took exception to the 'she' nomenclature. They lodged a formal complaint, a grievance, in the proper way using the proper process. It was all very public.

The manager's nightmare was complete when they learned that the potential financial penalties for discrimination are unlimited.

Well, question number one. What exactly is the grievance? Who is being harmed and in what way?

Then question number two. Does the grievance itself represent discriminatory behaviour by the women against the man?

Wait for it — question number three. If the manager upholds the grievance does making the man change the way he talks about himself represent discrimination?

Here is an example where a well-meaning law has now placed an employer in a serious catch-22 position. Not only was it

```
not of their making, it was almost impossible to predict
or avoid ahead of time.

So, what happened?
- The grievance was upheld and the man was asked not to do it
   again
- He appealed, claiming discrimination
- He went off sick with work-related stress
- The appeal, eventually heard in absentia, upheld the
   original verdict
- He resigned and lodged a claim for discrimination
- The client settled, before the employment tribunal, for an
   insignificant sum
- There was much angst all around
- The client repeated discrimination training for all staff
   and reasserted its credentials as an equal-opportunities
   environment
```

There are several learnings here:

- Perceptions of discrimination are different, subjective and highly emotional
- It's sometimes extremely difficult to see right from wrong
- Cool heads and friendly offline chats might have averted the issue but there is no guarantee that will work in every instance
- Although it was not the case here, you can see how easily malicious intent could create a very big problem out of very little

Just when you thought you were getting it...

DON'T

The risks of treating candidates differently

Our client runs a highly-automated factory employing highly-qualified technicians. When recruiting, he chooses CVs based on the qualifications and experience evident. He has a very long day of eight interviews. In the first seven he finishes the interview by saying 'we will get back to you in the next few days'. Even the ones he knew he would not employ. After the final interview, feeling very tired, he says 'sorry mate, but we won't be taking your application further'.

The disappointed candidate asks why, to be told that whilst his experience and qualifications were good, he didn't think he would be the right personality fit.

Candidate number eight was the only Asian interviewee.

It is said that people will judge you by your actions not your intentions. This was a moment like that.

Our client is unequivocal that his comment was not motivated by racial prejudice and he is absolutely clear that he did not intend to cause offence. He was simply 'choosing' a candidate based on the best behavioural style and skills fit he could find. This was not, in itself, unreasonable but it was open to interpretation. The simple fact remains this candidate was treated differently without showing clear evidence of an objective or justifiable reason. In such circumstances, intentions are irrelevant and each situation will be judged solely on the facts available. The key fact here was that no one else was given the same immediate and negative feedback so, therefore, there were no demonstrable grounds or discernible reasons to do so.

The candidate complained, asking how other candidates had been dealt with, and requesting copies of correspondence and CVs to satisfy himself he had not been unfairly treated. There was an implied but not expressed threat.

After a lot of activity (which took the manager away from his job while he addressed the situation), stress and masses of correspondence the candidate withdrew his complaint – or rather did not pursue it.

The lesson here is obvious. However well-intentioned you are as an employer, you must treat candidates in EXACTLY the same way, and in a fair and reasonable manner on all occasions.

On to our next example. Understandably, the law aims to protect pregnant females in the workplace. However, what if…

Understanding where the boundaries lie in employment law

This client is a large hairdressing salon. They are well known locally with an excellent reputation that has been hard won over a long period.

A female employee tells the owner she is pregnant. The forms are filled in and confinement dates are confirmed etc. The employee performs a combination of secondary functions as well as hairstyling and is customer facing.

She now starts to exhibit the following behaviours:
- She claims to feel poorly and leaves early, usually on Fridays or busy Saturdays
- She arrives late and unannounced, due to feeling poorly, and usually on Mondays

DON'T

- When customers, colleagues or the owner ask her challenging questions she responds 'you can't talk to me like that, I'm pregnant' causing distress and upsetting customers
- She picks and chooses what work and customers she will handle, but not on a consistent basis, causing disruption and discord for the other team members and the owner

Most of the team and customers are female. Many have been pregnant.

The owner genuinely does not want to cause the employee any stress. Equally she now has real issues to deal with.

The unspeakable truth is that everybody knew she was exploiting the situation and not playing fair. Undoubtedly though there were elements of truth and validity to some of her problems. It got to the point that many of the team wanted to confront her.

> I'M NOT SAYING THAT YOUR POST-NATAL DEPRESSION ISN'T REAL, MAUREEN, I'M JUST SAYING THAT YOUR SON IS NEARLY FIFTEEN!

As a business leader, where do you draw the line and, more importantly, *how* do you draw it?

There is no 'perfect' answer to that. The law does not make provision for managing people who choose to abuse the protection it is offering.

The only real answer is playing by the rules. There are rules around absence and lateness. Apply them as evenly as you would with anybody else, but apply them. When assignments are refused explore the reasons why. Make reasonable adjustments, if you can, or move to disciplinary measures if you feel there is no justification. If customers and team members are not being spoken to correctly, call it out and challenge the employee.

But, above all, whilst recognising the legal position, do not be intimidated into accepting unreasonable behaviours and attitudes.

Summary

Overall, our experience with discrimination in the work place is that we rarely find overtly bigoted employers. We overwhelmingly find employers and managers who are very keen to do the right thing and be seen to do so - even if they don't always understand what that means, or they fail to get it right.

If, as an employer, you are going to act in a prejudicial or discriminatory way then you are riding your luck. It is only a matter of time before somebody, quite rightly, will take exception to it. That could prove very expensive, stressful and damaging to your business and reputation. Worse of all, you might spend a huge amount of time trying to defend the indefensible. It is very unlikely that you will easily explain away why you asked a young woman about her plans for a family at interview, or expressed concern about somebody's request for help with stress in the work place, or wrote a job advert that obviously asked for a man, a 'young person' or made it very clear that you don't agree with certain religious or sexual preferences. We could go on. As an employer you know there is no excuse for this. It's just wrong.

However, there are many more situations in grey areas where the employer might find the right course of action unclear. Discrimination, like beauty, is in the eye of the beholder.

If I feel you are discriminating against me then that may just be enough to prompt me to take action against you, regardless of intent. For 'you' read any of your other employees, customers or suppliers – indeed anyone with whom you and people in your organisation come into contact. This is a very real business risk that needs to be fully understood and acknowledged by the employer if it is to be managed properly within the organisation.

Our experience tells us that there are no guaranteed ways to eliminate this risk entirely and there are always a very small minority of people who will actively exploit or create opportunities maliciously.

So, our insight would be:

- Be very consistent in your attitudes, behaviours and reactions towards people. Make sure your team do exactly the same and are equally sensitive, respectful and sincere in their dealings with *all* people
- Remember, it is no longer the case that you should 'treat others as you wish to be treated' but, 'treat others as *they* wish to be treated'

- Be aware of your own views and judgements and leave preconceived ideas, stereotypes and inbuilt prejudices at home
- Be alert and intuitive around things you see happening in your business and do not gloss over, or try to justify, repeated bad behaviours. Recognise them for what they are and stop them from happening
- Above all, let your personal approach be the beacon and the benchmark to which the whole organisation aspires

It also makes sense for organisations to monitor the diversity (including areas like ethnicity and disability) of its workforce, at every level, including during recruitment. So, for example, you should record the number of women who are making it into middle and senior level management roles. By tracking this data, it should be possible to obtain a clear picture of whether or not there is any potential discrimination or harassment taking place. Staff attitude surveys are also a valuable way of gathering feedback from people on their perceptions of the business in areas like gender equality in their workplace. It's in the interest of employers to not only eradicate discrimination in their businesses, but to develop proactive strategies for progressing talent wherever that may lie, so that they can reap the many benefits of having a truly diverse workforce.

Don't harass

Long gone are the days when bullies roamed free in the workplace but they are by no means extinct. They are alive and well but not 'free', and we now have the legal tools to define and curb that kind of behaviour as opposed to just 'sucking it up' and accepting it.

There are lots of different forms and causes of harassment.

Sometimes harassment is the natural toolkit of a bigot – the physical manifestation of behaviours designed to pick on people 'not like me'. They think that 'if I do it hard enough, for long enough, they will get out of my life'. You have probably seen individuals doing this, and thinking about those moments is likely to be making you cringe right now.

Other times it's cultural and more systemic. An office may believe, 'this is how we manage our people around here'. Wrapped up in euphemisms, it can be worn as a badge of honour:

- 'We don't suffer fools gladly.'
- 'Ours is a results-oriented culture.'
- 'There's no room for mediocrity.'
- 'We don't take prisoners.'
- 'We don't mince our words.'
- 'This is a tough environment.'
- 'Survival of the fittest.'
- 'I let them know who's the boss.'

Other times, it is the home of the incompetent. For example, 'if I am busy pushing you around then it's that much harder or downright unpleasant for you to expose my shortcomings'.

Whatever the driver, we usually see negative outcomes from harassment, organisationally. That does not necessarily mean that leads to change, because people are people, but sometimes these negative outcomes are really extreme and do force change.

We are not going to list the bad outcomes because we all know that bad management – and bullying is the epitome of bad management – produces rubbish results.

We also know that there is a world of difference between being given direction, encouragement, or even a 'telling off' from actually being bullied. Especially when the bullying is relentless. Our reactions to bullying are never positive. However, a true learning experience (a.k.a. a 'telling off') can actually be helpful. Knowing what the boss wants you to do, and by when, is motivating – even when it is communicated in a tough or exacting way.

Most importantly, a single 'thank you' or 'well done' from the boss on successfully completing that task goes a very long way to getting more out of you than any pointed finger.

Technically speaking, harassment in the workplace is defined under section 26 of the Equality Act 2010 as;

> *"unwanted conduct related to a relevant protected characteristic that has the purpose or effect of violating a person's dignity or creating an intimidating, hostile, degrading, humiliating or offensive environment for that person".*

And it is for the individual, not the employer, to decide if the treatment is offensive.

We have never come across an employer who has set out to deliberately harass or allow harassment to take place in their organisation. But it continues to happen and a 2017 study reported by the Chartered Institute of Personnel and Development (CIPD) indicated that 13% of employees reported that they had been the victim of harassment.

Harassment can and does present itself in different guises and can even amount to discrimination if it relates to one or more of the 'protected characteristics' set out under the Equality Act 2010. For example, sex, sexual orientation, gender reassignment, race (including colour, nationality, ethnic or national origins), religion or belief, disability or age.

It is also important to remember that employers will be vicariously liable for the unlawful acts of employees done in the course of employment, unless they can show that they took such steps as were *reasonably practicable* to prevent them.

Liability for harassment also extends to social functions that are connected with work such as a Christmas party or a drinks reception before a sales conference. This is the case even if the event is out of hours. That clears that up then.

Often, we find that companies assume that they don't have a problem with harassment in their organisation because they haven't received any formal complaints. The reality is that harassment can be 'hidden' and unless employers are clear about their view of what is acceptable and unacceptable behaviour in their workplace and are willing to act when they see it, victims might be reluctant to come forward.

So, typically we deal with 'shocked' employers who will say that 'this has never happened in our company before'. Really? A lack of previous complaints is not the scale by which to measure and once the issue surfaces, it is often the tip of a very large iceberg which the organisation has skillfully learned to navigate around.

Another key factor in harassment being a 'hidden' issue is that those responsible for the harassment are selective and subtle in the manner and form that they harass their victims. They choose them carefully to ensure they are the most vulnerable. For example, they are usually the youngest, oldest or newest etc. They also harass when there are no witnesses to the harassment or when no one is likely to come forward on the victim's behalf.

Inevitably it is not just the victim of harassment that loses out, but ultimately so does the business.

```
When harassment is 'hidden' by managers wanting to maintain
    control

A very sad example from our experience occurred where a
    capable and engaged operations manager who was highlighted
     for promotion suddenly stopped performing and started
    taking time off work sick.

It took some time for the employer to connect this to the
    appointment of a new operations director.

The operations manager's previous boss recognised his
    potential. He had coached and developed him and given him
    opportunities to progress. The new operations director saw
     the operations manager as a threat and was determined to
    'keep him in his place'. He was not overt in doing so, but
     constantly called the operations manager to his office
    where behind closed doors he would criticise and
    countermand the manager's decisions. He also undermined
    his authority by calling meetings with the manager's team
    in his absence and changing instructions without reference
     to him.
```

DON'T

The operations director had a nickname for everyone and called the operations manager 'the hairdresser' and intimated that he was gay due to his choice of car and because the manager dressed smartly in a coordinated shirt and tie and looked after his general appearance.

The manager did not make any complaint as he felt that to do so would be 'making a fuss' or being over-sensitive. Besides, he wanted to prove himself to his new boss.

It was not until the manager was absent due to depression and work-based stress that the employer really took a close look at what was in plain sight and spoke to the manager about what had taken place.

Even with the knowledge of what had occurred, the employer did not do anything in relation to the operations director's behaviour.

Sadly, the manager left the organisation so they lost a loyal, previously effective and motivated employee.

The company chose to take the view that, as there had been no formal complaint, there wasn't an issue and, on this occasion, they were lucky that the matter did not result in an employment tribunal claim.

However, following the appointment of a new operations manager some months later it was déjà vu already.

This time the new incumbent was less willing to tolerate this behaviour and left after one year lodging a claim at the employment tribunal. Among other complaints he asserted that the operations director's behaviour constituted sexual harassment on the basis of his perceived sexual orientation. Other members of the workforce also then came forward to support the operations manager's complaints on the basis that they found the operations director's behaviour unacceptable.

As before, when approached the operations director denied any form of harassment saying that he was trying to help the operations manager by 'toughening him up for the real world' and that his intentions were entirely genuine. Sadly, the employer did not realise that the motive of the harasser is irrelevant. It is very dangerous to assume that the individual who is the target of the harassment is over-reacting or over-sensitive.

It is the individual's perception that is important and whether or not it is reasonable to assume that the behaviour would have the effect it did. It is the notion of creating an offensive environment that is key. In this particular instance the claimant won his claim. And so did his colleagues. Interesting to note it was not necessary for the behaviour complained of to be directed at the other individuals for such behaviour to be found to be unlawful and discriminatory. Now there's a scary lesson.

When we began to work with the employer, he had recently settled the tribunal case which had been an expensive and highly emotional experience. He had not realized that awards for claims for acts of discrimination are unlimited and include compensation for 'injury to feelings' which, at the time of writing, can range from £900 to £44,000 or more in some instances.

He was at a loss as to what had happened and how he could prevent it happening again. He felt that the whole system was against him. The fact is, he was not the victim, and there were some very basic and necessary steps he should have taken. So we helped him to put them in place.

- Firstly, he needed to set out a clear and unambiguous statement of the company's view on harassment and bullying in the form of a policy. This informed all employees that such conduct would not be tolerated and that it amounted to misconduct.

- We then helped him to develop a well-publicised complaints procedure that allowed all individuals to raise complaints confidentially and without fear of recrimination.

- Both the policy and procedure were communicated to every employee through a series of short training sessions.

- Finally, we impressed upon him the need to follow-up with action – courageous action. In this instance, the operations director was taken through procedure and dismissed.

- So, this particular employer went from zero to hero by simply paying attention to problems which he had previously turned a blind eye to or had placed on the 'too difficult' pile.

In terms of litigation, it is *always* easier, quicker and cheaper to resolve matters as soon as they arise. The cost to everyone involved grows in direct proportion to the length of time the issues are ignored or tolerated. Collusion is never the solution!

Now, harassment can take many forms as I'm sure you will have seen. The three main categories are verbal, physical and sexual harassment.

Verbal harassment

Verbal harassment is where the boss or a colleague says things in an aggressive, suggestive, ridiculing or offensive way.

Verbal harassment can be many things. It might be crude, sophisticated, emotional or psychological. It can be one syllable delivered in a north-country accent or an extract of the Oxford English Dictionary from an ex-public school boy. The effect is likely the same. Verbal harassment is a very common form of harassment and we see more of it than we might like to.

The word 'banter' is often used as some kind of excuse or explanation. Let's have a look at this next example that explores this phenomenon in more detail.

```
Religious discrimination, bullying and harassment

Three shop floor members of a client's assembly plant business
    were accused of carrying out a sustained campaign of
    bullying towards a colleague who had openly expressed his
    strongly held Christian beliefs.

The three men routinely called him names such as 'the bible
    basher' and 'Moses' and would sing 'Jesus wants me for a
    sunbeam' whenever he walked across the shop floor, often
    replacing the actual words of the song with their own
    colourful versions.

Matters finally came to a head when, to 'celebrate' his
    birthday, the three men tied the employee to a chair and
    suspended a cross above his head in a mock crucifixion.
    They left him in the canteen so that everyone taking a
    break would see him.
```

> This came to the attention of management and we were called in to help investigate. During interviews, the three men consistently denied having behaved inappropriately, dismissing their actions as 'just a bit of banter'. We suspected that, secretly, this was also the view of some of the managers. How else could the situation have arisen? Why had the earlier 'banter' not been challenged and stopped?
>
> When the details were examined, it was clear that, far from being light-hearted or fun, this was an assault by three employees on their colleague and one which had put him in fear of violence by harassment.
>
> The upshot was that all three employees were summarily dismissed. However, not before we had a very 'lively' discussion with the owner of the business in which we had to work hard to persuade him that we were not being overly harsh in our findings.
>
> He was incredulous when we explained that there were actually rules around this kind of behaviour. Yes, truly. He was also stunned when we told him that we routinely carried out anti-harassment and bullying training with organisations. What he actually said was 'you're telling me that people actually pay to have training in how to behave at work? F****** ridiculous!!'

If you think this case is extreme then think again. A recent nationwide poll found that one in eight employees has experienced harassment and even violence of one form or another in the workplace which the perpetrators have tried to brush aside as 'banter' or 'having a laugh'.

It is a startling fact but, in many instances, we have found that the employers themselves do not recognise the inappropriateness of such behaviour. If we only had a tenner for every time we've been told 'it's just a bit of harmless fun', 'if you can't take the heat, stay out of the kitchen' or 'you don't understand, this is how it is in the "real" world'.

However, in the real world such a lack of response from management to banter is a complete abdication of responsibility and duty and, frankly, just ain't right. It's no good just writing policies about having a 'duty of care'. Unless appropriate and acceptable behaviour is actually demonstrated by managers on a day-by-day basis, policies are not worth the paper they are written on.

Perhaps the most important lesson learned is the need to clearly establish the line between 'banter' and behaviours that, if left unchecked, become corrosive. In practice, this means being vigilant in the workplace and correcting inappropriate language and behaviour on a conversation-by-conversation basis.

Which brings us on to the related area of physical harassment...

Physical harassment

Physical harassment can be anything from invading your private space or throwing things around the office, to assault. It can be accompanied by loud verbal harassment. If it is a one off and there's little damage caused it's probably forgivable. If it is sustained as a 'proven' management technique by bosses, or if it's allowed to carry on generally around the workplace you are likely, at best, to lose good people or, at worst, to create a hostile environment encouraging violence and disrespect.

As you'll see from this next example it can also be hidden in plain sight under the mask of 'fun'.

DON'T

The dangers of 'horseplay'

Our client, a large engineering firm, was long established and traditionally run with, we thought, some comical ideas like the 'hourly paid canteen' and the 'management dining room'.

The factory floor staff started as apprentices and learned their trade over four years from their elders and a bit of college work. In truth, they were genuinely building a skilled work force.

However, it was common practice at key stages of the apprenticeship for 'rituals' to be enacted upon the unsuspecting trainees in the manner of university initiation ceremonies or US college hazing. You can guess what they were. We don't need to paint pictures that keep you awake at night.

Management at all levels, including the board, saw it as 'part and parcel' of the trainees' experience and hadn't thought to tell us about these 'rituals', even though it could be interpreted as physical abuse of employees.

Now this was all conceived long before (yes, you guessed it) the arrival of social media. Clearly, details of this sort of stuff are readily made public now.

So, here we were, having not been previously made aware of the customs performed upon the apprentices, when the client calls to say 'what do I do now?'

About 24 hours after the first photos were posted, the phone started to ring. It was all getting very embarrassing and potentially costly. Now it was in the public domain it didn't look quite so much fun.

This was followed by a large amount of damage limitation, as well as ignorance pleading and blame attribution by the company.

It was stupid, dangerous and highly damaging to their generally well-deserved reputation as a trainer and employer. This was an employer that was growing very quickly and struggling to meet demand with its current work force levels so any bad press was highly damaging to its ability to grow sustainably.

> I CAN ASSURE YOU THAT OUTDATED INITIATION RITES HAVE NO PLACE IN THIS MODERN, FORWARD LOOKING COMPANY.

Old-fashioned rites of passage or 'horseplay' are very unlikely to fit the modern workplace. Overly zealous attempts to 'celebrate' employee successes are potentially counter-productive. Being young, junior or a trainee should not give older, more experienced or time-served individuals any exemptions from decent behaviour. Just because it happened to them 'back in the day' does not make it acceptable.

Sexual harassment

We are now going to venture into the oldest and yet, in some ways, the newest form of harassment as the law tries to play catch up. It has obviously been going on forever. The 'casting couch' is a well-known expression for a reason.

However, defining it and developing rules around it is not quite as simple as it sounds.

When is sexual discrimination actually sexual harassment – or vice versa?

The old stereotype of a male boss harassing a female junior is far too simplistic a definition in our modern world that is still struggling to give a name to all of the sexualities it is looking to give respect to. Therefore, an employer's areas of responsibility or 'risk zones' are many more than might be obvious.

At what point does joking become harassing? Define, *universally*, the point where a bit of banter becomes sexual harassment. It may be true that 'if it offends' it is harassment. But how do you know the 'offence threshold' of every individual in a room?

The same difficulty arises with hugs, air kisses, hands on shoulders or just getting too close to someone. Even an overlong handshake might be seen as 'going too far' for some people.

The law is obviously well meaning but some people may find this uncertainty over what constitutes harassment difficult to interpret and feel it curbs the spontaneity and personality of their workplace. However, there needs to be awareness and sympathy towards people's boundaries to ensure everyone in that workplace feels safe and listened to.

Here is an example that is quite complex:

```
Malicious misrepresentation in sexual harassment complaints

The outcome is true and absolutely mind boggling. If you are a
    CEO you might find it blood chilling. If not, you might
    see it as a lesson in 'how to'.

The client was a family-owned business managed by a
    professional board  led by a CEO who was not part of the
    family. The non-executive chairman was family and they had
    'their man' on the board in the form of the financial
    director who was virtually fireproof. The family are
    otherwise absent, save for their desire for dividends.

The business had been struggling and the relatively new CEO
    was leading a change programme to restore earnings growth.

Change programmes are often difficult for staff as they
    invariably mean changes which they don't necessarily like
    or benefit from. This can cause challenges for HR teams.

This programme was financially successful and achieved
    substantially improved results. But, along the way, the FD
    and his direct report, the HR manager, were severely
```

tested by these changes and found wanting by the CEO. They felt that their jobs may be under threat and they worried that the CEO held all the cards.

The CEO is now on holiday for two weeks.

Just prior to his break, he'd chaired a particularly 'fruity' sales meeting. He used some direct, ill-judged words to motivate his team, including encouraging them 'not to be like a load of bloody old women'. There was a female sales team member in the room.

You know what's coming. It's crystal clear. But it happened.

She raised a formal complaint. The HR manager - in consultation with the FD and chairman - felt it appropriate to immediately suspend the CEO. He was on holiday so this was completely inappropriate. They then began an investigation into that complaint and solicited, from female staff, any instances they felt the CEO behaved 'inappropriately'. A small catalogue of incidents was compiled including:
- 'He stands too close to me.'
- 'He stands behind me when he is reading things on my computer screen.'
- 'He arranges to stay in the same hotel at the same time as other female staff do when travelling on business.'
- 'He offered to take a very distressed female staff member for a coffee off-site to help her calm down.'

These, along with the sales meeting issue, were deemed indictment enough by the chairman to summarily dismiss the CEO. Unsurprisingly, he appealed and it was settled with an appropriate payment.

Whilst the politics are obvious, the family was not best served by this — imposing their own political motives rather than engaging in fair behaviour was costly. However neither was the CEO's reputation enhanced as he had left himself vulnerable to criticism.

Malicious misrepresentation can happen, and managers need to be vigilant about loose terms, especially in moments of high tension. Moreover, being the boss no longer affords the cover to be careless in the way you engage with people. You need to operate to a professional standard at all times and developing clear, neutral motivational vocabulary for the modern workplace is an essential skill that is mandatory not optional.

Offensive behaviour, banter and bad language

Consider the 2019 case of a police officer dismissed from her post following a string of inappropriate behaviours including breaking wind in her police station and using the C-word repeatedly.

The detective constable admitted to passing wind outside the sergeant's office after she was summoned to a disciplinary hearing where she revealed "it wasn't deliberate", the Sun newspaper reported.

She also confessed to using foul language while on duty, but claimed it was part of the 'culture of banter' at the station. She said "I would joke about it. Sometimes I would speak like the character Borat or use a silly voice to say 'rather out than in'."

On another occasion, the officer who was working on a temporary basis, also asked a junior officer if he wanted an affair with a 'fatter, ugly, older woman'. Fellow

    officers also witnessed the detective constable yell at a
    motorist "you're driving like a c***", before arresting
    the man.

  Overall, she was accused of 25 counts of unprofessional
    behaviour between summer and December 2017. Following a
    disciplinary hearing, she was dismissed from her duties,
    and the force where she had worked for 22 years.

The law is quite clear in defining the consequences of behaviour that crosses 'red lines' in terms of language and behaviour. It's there to protect people who work in and around the organisation including those in positions of authority. The requirements of the legislation need to be articulated in a written policy that spells out exactly where the 'red lines' of behaviour (verbal or non-verbal) sit and, also, what will happen to *anyone* who crosses those lines. Training then breathes life into the policy and gives everyone a first-hand understanding of how closely (or otherwise) their own behaviour mirrors that required by the organisation.

This is not 'overkill' or being too politically correct. It is now a key commercial imperative that protects the organisation, and the people within it, from unacceptable and potentially contentious behaviours. Again, beauty and offence lie in the eye the beholder and simply treating others as you wish to be treated is no longer appropriate. The key is to treat others in the way that *they* wish to be treated as prevention is always better, and cheaper, than cure.

Harassment of the boss

When we think about harassment or bullying in the workplace there is often an assumption that this is likely to be employer to employee or employee to employee. But, what about when an employee or employees bully or harass their boss?

This is probably more common than you'd imagine and we've dealt with a number of instances over the years. When this does happen, regardless of the business sector, scale of business or circumstances (and these do differ widely), there are always a number of common factors present.

Firstly, there is no (or a poor) understanding of boundaries. By boundaries we mean:

- Relationship boundaries which result in casual, unguarded behaviour – which is fundamentally different to simply informal behaviour
- Role and role responsibility boundaries which result in a lack of understanding of what is reasonably expected of individuals and what they should reasonably expect from the organisation
- Boundaries of authority. Who is actually 'running the show'?

Secondly, the manager or owner has little or no formal understanding of what constitutes a balanced working relationship and often lacks any managerial or leadership training.

Finally, and this really is the most common factor, the manager or owner acts out of a genuine desire to foster good working relationships with their people, and treat them well. But the staff do not reciprocate.

When these factors combine the results are messy, distressing, hugely expensive and time-consuming to untangle. Here is a typical example of the situations we encounter.

DON'T

Harassment can occur upwards, downwards and peer-to-peer

- The new owner of an old, established but unprofitable coffee shop and bistro was energised with enthusiasm and determined to run the business successfully. He met with all of his staff as a group, and then spent time on a one-to-one basis getting to know them and sharing his plans to reinvigorate the business and create a great work environment.

So far, so good.

- However, from the initial meetings, it became apparent that the previous owner had put no effort into the running of the business. Her approach had been 'casual', leaving staff to muddle through without any sense of direction about what was to be achieved.

- As a result, staff had little or no feel for the identity of the business, who its customers were, or who they should target and what they should be offering. They had no sense of where they were heading. There was no role structure or organisation as to who did what on a day-to-day basis and each shift was more like a comedy of errors rather than a well-choreographed performance.

- It also emerged that two members of staff (one of whom was designated as a manager and the other her deputy) had been running the operation to suit their own personal circumstances. They informed the new owner that they would only work certain hours on certain days and that there were jobs that were too demeaning for them to carry out. From the accounts of other staff, they 'ruled the junior staff with a rod of iron', and a number of complaints began to emerge about their bullying.

EMPLOYMENT LAW IS NOT FOR THE CONVENIENCE OF EMPLOYERS

This whole exercise, designed to motivate and inspire staff members about the future of the business, caused the new owner to become anxious about what he had taken on. He was conflicted about what to do next.

This was a classic case of a lack of boundaries. The business had been a 'vanity project' for the previous owner. As long as the staff didn't bother her, they could do as they pleased. The fact that the business wasn't making money didn't seem to be an issue.

Based on his previous experience and with a misguided sense that if he 'played nicely', so would his staff, the new owner tried to rectify matters.

He started by discussing job descriptions and roles with the staff including the manager and her deputy. This was welcomed by all of the staff other than the two managers who didn't want anything to change.

Two significant events then happened. Firstly, the two managers challenged the new owner – 'who did he think he was to say how things should work?'. Secondly, they tried to rally the rest of the staff to object to the imposition of job roles. This was a classic result of 'casual' work relationships.

The owner tried to calm the situation by sitting down and listening to the complaints from the manager and her deputy. His intention was to have an amicable and rational conversation, but this quickly descended into a series of threats and accusations by the managers. They said they were going to ACAS (Advisory, Conciliation and Arbitration Service) for advice as they did not like the way he delivered information, labelling him a 'dictator'.

This situation was further complicated by the fact that the

owner had to address the allegations of harassment and bullying put forward by junior members of staff. Quite rightly, the owner proceeded with caution to investigate the grievances as was proper.

Within days the new owner found himself in the middle of a maelstrom. The two managers fought him constantly over their job roles, working hours and payment. They demanded a bonus even though the business had been losing money consistently for a year. They were actively trying to rally the staff against him even though three colleagues had made formal grievances of harassment and bullying against both managers. There was even a formal complaint from a customer who had booked a private event, which the manager had failed to communicate to anyone else, resulting in 24 disgruntled guests.

When the owner attempted to impose some form of order, via a formal investigation, one of the managers went off sick alleging work-based stress. Via her solicitor, she also filed a formal complaint of bullying and harassment against the owner.

By this stage the owner was reeling and he himself was suffering from work-based stress. He wasn't eating or sleeping and was fast approaching the stage where he was afraid to say anything to anybody in case it resulted in more claims and accusations.

So, what did he do wrong? Or, more importantly, what could he have done to avoid the melodrama?

Firstly, he needed to set out clear **relationship boundaries** to avoid the development of casual behaviour. From the outset, he should have been clear about what his staff should expect from him and what he expected from them including the way they should deal with each other.

Informality is fine but this does not mean being casual. Respectfulness is key to setting and understanding relationship boundaries. This includes respect for the individual, respect for the roles people play as well as respectfulness in attitudes and behaviour towards one another.

The owner needed to literally spell out the difference between informal and casual behaviour by giving his team clear examples to illustrate his point. For example, a key lesson is how staff members should address each other and what is permissible in terms of language used. This business is customer-facing and bad language or slang is not professional. Shouting across rooms to each other is not acceptable, nor is holding personal conversations in front of guests or within their earshot. Using a quiet tone is required, along with demonstrating patience and understanding at all times.

Secondly, he needed to be clear about **role and role responsibility boundaries.** He assumed that because his was a small organisation and because people had worked there for some time that they would already be clear about who did what and how. But this simply does not happen by accident. It is not just about putting job profiles in place, although this is a good start. It's about defining the most significant parts of each role and how they fit together to make the whole organisation work effectively. It's about how much time and effort should be put into the different aspects of the role and at what point the incumbent needs to refer upwards when their expertise or authority is exceeded.

This leads to the need to clearly define **boundaries of authority.** Who is actually 'running the show'? In this age of employee engagement and empowerment, employers too often defer to their staff on matters which they should be deciding.

That is not to say that involvement is not important but there is a major difference between delegation and abdication of responsibility. In this instance, instead of setting out where the boundaries were for determining strategy and the direction of the business, the owner was trying to run it by committee. A better approach would have been to seek involvement from the staff and consult on changes and then for the owner to make his decision and inform them rather than seek their permission.

This may have led to some 'difficult conversations' but better that these are addressed and resolved early on than putting them off until they become almost insurmountable barriers. This is important, not just for the owner, but for the majority of his staff who want to move on with the business.

Summary

So, what have we learned?

The first thing is that this is becoming a problem for employers more frequently than you might think.

Secondly, when dealing with harassment at work, prevention is always better than cure. All too often employers seem to dodge the issue or try to downplay incidents, perhaps because they don't want to cause offence or be seen as a killjoy. This just allows the issue to grow which creates confusion by giving out mixed messages to staff. Employees recognise that what happens in practice is not what might be written in the policies and procedures and they lose respect for those individuals with the authority to set the right standards and prevent unacceptable behaviour.

The key is to engage with staff directly and set out a clear, zero-tolerance standard for unacceptable behaviour. Over the last few months, most visibly in the #MeToo and Time's Up movements, there has been a huge push-back from female employees in different industries (including high profile sectors such as film and entertainment) regarding sexual harassment. This is the beginning of a sea-change in attitudes towards unacceptable behaviour of all kinds. This, alongside growing awareness of concepts of employee wellbeing, mean that expectations are likely to transform the workplace of the future. Hopefully to one that is free from hostility and based on tolerance, where people can make their best contribution without fear of harassment or bullying.

Organisations should also strive to develop a culture in which harassment is known to be unacceptable and where individuals are confident enough to bring complaints without fear of ridicule or reprisal. Organisations should deal promptly, seriously and discreetly with any issues that are raised.

So, our insights would be:

- Prevention is always better than cure (and cheaper!)
- Give staff a clear, zero-tolerance standard for acceptable and unacceptable behaviour
- Encourage people to feel confident in coming forward if they experience harassment
- Take it seriously and deal promptly and discreetly with any issues raised

Don't underpay

The minimum wage and the national living wage are well-established bottom lines for paying staff in the UK. We don't really want to focus on this, but we will give you some warnings around common 'mistakes' when employers are found to have underpaid, such as:

- using tips to top-up low basic pay
- misunderstanding staff deductions for things like uniforms or accommodation
- miscalculating actual hours worked with irregular or zero-hour contracts
- lack of clarity on travel to work time with multi-location operations

What we want to focus on is 'equal pay' as this is the key area of responsibility and risk for managers.

Quite properly, in our view, the law aims to create fairness in workers' pay. Some people hold a different view that if people are prepared to do the work for that rate of pay then where's the harm?

This opinion becomes morally dubious if the only reasons for differentiation are sex or age. But it's not the argument we want to have right now.

If the law says that you cannot pay different rates of pay to people of different sexes then it should be easy enough for employers to sort that out.

We are at the start of a period of further exposure and transparency that will help to clear the murky picture on equal pay for women until something close to equality prevails. If your organisation has this problem it ain't going away. Reputations are going to get shredded. Employers have no other robust option than to resolve it – sooner rather than later.

Critically, this means:

Employers are obliged to pay all workers the same rate of pay for work of the same *value*.

Of course, this isn't as simple as it sounds. It's obviously easy to measure pay for a like-for-like job – for example, a cleaner in Swansea and a cleaner in Leeds – easy.

But, does my accountant do work of the same value as my sales manager? Does the skilled factory technician do the same value work as the maintenance engineer?

The complications with this kind of issue are fourfold:

1. Any claim of unequal pay can be backdated indefinitely
2. Claims will require rigorous defence by the employer which are costly, distracting and stressful, although you can suggest settling out of court
3. The only real way to avoid claims in the future is to implement a job evaluation scheme that will define, on record, the comparative value of each role. But this is expensive and provides very limited added value to the employer beyond this functionality
4. It is very difficult to account for market forces driving unbalanced rates of pay, i.e. a sales manager in London earning more than a sales manager in Birmingham

Once again, the employer can be forgiven for thinking employment law is nigh on impossible to comply with.

And, what if you only employ women in the low-paid jobs and men in the higher-paid jobs? Is that not flouting the spirit of the law?

Reports on the gender pay gap in large employers are exposing this exact situation. Just look at the mess the BBC got in over this, with some high-profile presenters offering to take massive pay cuts to even things up. Then there were the big financial houses in London where the big money was earned by men because – yes, they really said this – the talent pool for those jobs had too few women to go around the whole industry.

There is much confusion among employees (and HR departments) about the difference between unequal pay and the gender pay gap. Equal pay refers to work of equal value whereas the gender pay gap refers to the difference in the average earnings of men and women. There are a variety of factors behind it, including the impact on women's career progression of taking time out of the labour market to have children, and career choices, with typical "male" subjects such as IT and science often leading to higher-paid roles.

To address the issue, the government introduced a requirement for all large organisations to publish their gender pay gap.

More than 10,000 employers published gender pay gap data for the first time in 2018, covering businesses with 250+ employees. Our view is that this kind of reporting is only going to go in one direction. That means the inclusion of smaller and, eventually, *all* businesses, regardless of size. In fact, just under 6% of smaller employers already reported on a voluntary basis in 2018. Executive pay gap reporting was introduced from January 2019 and, at the time of writing, consultations are under way for the introduction of ethnic pay gap reporting. The recommendations from the Matthew Taylor report on the modern workplace has set a direction of travel that is moving towards greater transparency, parity and equality across all sectors and sections of employment.

It's not just about asking whether you have a gender pay gap in your business, but why you have that gap and, most importantly, what you are going to do about it.

So, what can you do?

The first thing is to do the maths. Regardless of the reason, do you pay men and women, on average, more or less money (note there are some statistical gymnastics to master but let's not get distracted). Remember, if you have more than 250 employees you are obliged to do this.

Then you can start to ask *why* and decide *what* you are going to do about it.

This may seem like a complicated and unnecessary thing to do but, trust us, when your company does fall within those required to publish their gender pay gap information you will be eternally thankful that you got ahead of the game. Remember, when required to do so, you will have to publish this information on your own website *and* on a government website and current and potential employees will have the opportunity to compare your treatment of workers with other companies.

As ever, there are consequences for employers if they fail to comply with their gender pay gap reporting obligations. Both for failing to comply (this will constitute an "unlawful act" within the meaning of s.34 of the Equality Act 2006, which empowers the Equality and Human Rights Commission (EHRC) to take enforcement action) and in being publicly 'named and shamed'.

So, the message is clear. Get ahead of the game. Understand the reporting requirements and run these over your own organisation now, while you still have time to address any gaps and create your *own* action plan rather than having this imposed.

The Gender Pay Gap

A client has a diverse workforce in a manufacturing environment. Traditionally there had been a cohort of male operatives with longer service and higher skillsets who were paid on average more than the female workers in the organisation. However, in order to address a potential long term embarrassment they have increased all workers pay and registered with the Living Wage Foundation.

The cost to the employer in this instance was relatively minor but the impact on the workforce was disproportionately positive.

Summary

For many reasons, it isn't a good idea to short change employees in relation to the National Minimum Wage by blurring pay with other aspects of employment. It's going to become increasingly awkward to have a significant and ongoing difference in the average pay of men and women and whether you can justify that or not may prove irrelevant to the reputational damage it causes.

Don't avoid the paperwork

Boring, boring boring...... we know.

But, there is no excuse for not doing the paperwork. You can get most forms, like contracts and handbooks, free from the internet. If you cannot find them there are more than enough HR professionals to go around. Once the few essential forms are complete, keeping them up-to-date is easy.

More importantly, without paperwork what fills the void? Well, history, fiction, guesswork and, at best, good intentions if you are lucky. Or deliberate mischief if not. Even if everyone has good intentions there are bound to be misunderstandings over what is expected of employees as people can forget or misinterpret.

All employees are legally entitled to a contract of employment which should include their:

- job title, who they report to and their main duties
- rate of pay and other benefits
- hours and location of work
- holiday entitlement
- sick pay entitlement
- notice period
- period of probation, if appropriate
- start date
- requirement to read the employee handbook

In an offer letter, or email, you can cover these in a Statement of Main Terms.

The employee handbook is the rule book. It's like the rules of membership of a social club.

How can you fairly judge somebody's behaviour if you have not told them what the standard of behaviour should be? That's all a handbook does, along with telling employees what might happen if they break the rules, and how they can complain if they think you or others are breaking the rules.

Now, we fully accept working out those rules can be a bit of a challenge. What is my company car policy? What is my dress code? What is my sickness policy? What will I do if they are continually absent? What is the sanction for being late?

But if you don't do this you can't be surprised if they behave in ways you don't like.

An employee handbook can be particularly useful if you end up in dispute or even at a tribunal. Any reasonable person looking at the facts is searching for a reference point. If it's not there you are effectively in a lottery as to whether a tribunal will find in favour of you, as the employer, or the employee.

Keeping files up-to-date is just as important. If you train employees, record it on file. If you discipline employees, record it on file. If employees are absent or late – you guessed it – record it on file.

If you change a person's role, rate of pay or major terms of employment, write it down and put it on file. It is the only way to be sure of the facts in the future when one of you 'misremembers'.

The stakes recently got higher. Since the introduction of the General Data Protection Regulation (GDPR) in May 2018, record keeping has become mandatory for all employers.

This includes a clear company policy on the handling and storage of personal data, including how long you will retain it for and the legal purpose for holding it, and the all-important requirement to actually record the data in the first place. If there's no legal basis for holding the data, or that basis ceases to apply, you must delete it.

It's worth setting out a company policy so everyone knows the standard retention period for each type of data and you can avoid non-compliance with GDPR.

Here are the kind of staff records you need to retain, by law.

- Right to work in the UK
- Pay rate records to meet the statutory requirement to issue workers with pay statements and to ensure you are paying your workers national minimum wage
- Terms and conditions of employment including a copy of each employee's written statement and correspondence relating to any changes to their terms and conditions
- Payroll records on Income Tax and National Insurance deductions for HM Revenue and Customs
- Sickness of more than four days and how much statutory sick pay you have paid
- Accidents, injuries and dangerous occurrences to meet health and safety requirements
- You must also keep records to ensure that weekly working time and night work limits (under the Working Time Regulations) are complied with in your business. It's up to you to determine what records you need to keep for these purposes, but you may be able to use existing records such as pay

It's also good practice to keep records for each worker including:

- Training and appraisals
- Employment history i.e. start date, promotions and job titles
- Personal details i.e. name, address, emergency phone numbers, qualifications and work-relevant disabilities

It's important to keep these records:

- Written records of meetings, such as minutes, with workplace representatives
- Any 'live' disciplinary warnings and/or sanctions
- Individual and collective redundancy consultation meetings and agreements
- Negotiations relating to information and consultation agreements

When you no longer need to keep data, it must be disposed of securely and effectively, for example by shredding hard copies and comprehensive IT deletion, including email history. Where possible, make data on workers and former workers anonymous.

Failure to delete records when you no longer have legitimate grounds to retain them can result in hefty fines. Under GDPR the Information Commissioner's Office can impose fines for serious breaches up to €20 million or 4% of the organisation's total worldwide annual turnover of the preceding financial year, whichever is higher.

Despite these risks, if you don't keep the necessary records it is almost impossible to lodge a defence against any complaint made by an employee or ex-employee so it is hugely beneficial to your business in the long run.

Here are a couple of examples that serve as a reminder of what can

DON'T

happen when employers fail to record.

Failing to identify and record an existing medical condition

This relates to an employer who failed to record an employee's induction progress. Despite having a clear policy that this would take place, and a format for doing so, the employer was simply 'too busy'.

Unfortunately, the employee did not make good progress and neither the line manager nor director noted the poor performance of the individual or take note of her circumstances. After eight weeks, dissatisfied with her attendance at work, the employer terminated her employment.

Shortly afterwards, the employer received an employment tribunal claim on the basis of disability discrimination. Stunned, the employer could not understand how this could have happened.

There was no record made by her manager on commencement of her employment that the employee had depression; an existing medical condition that constituted a disability. Nor was there any record of the 'return to work' conversation that took place between the employee and her manager, early in her employment, when she had failed to attend work. During this conversation she had informed her employer that she had been suffering with a bad stomach due to IBS.

While the employee did not use the words 'stress-related' in this conversation, had the employer made a record of the original declaration and recorded the 'return to work' conversation, the two may have been linked and action taken to investigate the reasons for absence in the context of a disability.

The employer was reasonably expected to have done so and, as they did not, they found themselves on the losing end of a claim for disability discrimination that cost them several thousand pounds.

Failing to fully document the terms of a secondment

A second example relates to a situation where an employee had been placed on secondment for an extended period of eighteen months. At the end of the period, the employer wanted the employee to move back to their original role which was a slightly less senior position. The employee refused saying that the move was permanent and that, if the role was no longer there, they should be made redundant. The employer insisted that the current role had only ever been a temporary secondment.

This resulted in a difficult and protracted dispute that led to the breakdown of the working relationship which ultimately became untenable. The employer ended up paying a settlement to the employee to avoid employment tribunal proceedings. They also lost an employee who had previously been a loyal and effective member of the team.

The learnings here are clear. Always put the secondment agreement in writing, both as a company policy and an individual, signed agreement. Set out the terms for pay, annual leave, sickness, absence and family leave as well as making it clear that the employee has ongoing employment with the original employer. Finally, define how and when the arrangement will end and what will happen to the employee within the organisation.'

Summary

Without proper records it's near impossible to manage in a fair and consistent manner. If you get into dispute they are your evidence, without them you have no defence. Additionally, if your people don't know where they stand, how do you expect them to conform?

Do

Here we focus on areas where it pays for managers to be proactive. We cover three key suggestions which will help you to manage your employees fairly and effectively:

- Do play fair
- Do remember who's the boss
- Do listen and watch

Do play fair

There are lots of ways to play unfairly as an employer. Here are just a few.

You can write contractual terms that are ridiculously biased in your favour. One of the worst examples of this is 'exclusive' zero-hour contracts. Zero-hour contracts can have a good and legitimate role in the workplace. Employees who need flexibility, such as students, single parents and carers, meet employers who need flexibility. But, if the flexibility is all one way then it's no way to build a relationship, or a business for that matter. Saying they can only work for you, but you can't guarantee them any work, or that they must come in when you call, but you can't guarantee them hours, is simply ridiculous and will be your downfall. The road to loyalty is a two-way street.

Similarly, expecting team members to pay for your business expenses is just not right. Clauses around costs for uniforms, training qualifications, stationery, tips, mobile phones, tools and safety equipment need to be balanced and genuinely reasonable. Would it feel fair if applied to you?

Requiring staff to work excessive, unsociable hours or do large amounts of unpaid time or overtime is a very common caper.

The old 'on call' ruse is a great way to get 'free' cover from employees.

Putting in bonus or commissions earnings that you do not intend to pay by calling it 'discretionary' is lying.

Being ambiguous about reporting structures or job responsibilities because it is a bit awkward to say the truth in writing is papering over cracks and leaves you exposed if they perform badly.

Having policies and procedures that put a ridiculous onus on the employee is not as unusual as you might think.

Playing fairly can extend more widely into how people are treated on a human level. The old adage that you should treat people how you would like to be treated is, as we have said several times already, not quite right. You should treat them how *they* expect to be treated. Without raking over discrimination or harassment again it is very easy to expose the organisation legally by treating people inconsistently or inappropriately. Sometimes even with the best of intentions as this next example shows.

EMPLOYMENT LAW IS NOT FOR THE CONVENIENCE OF EMPLOYERS

Exercising management discretion

The managing director of a small professional services business had all the necessary contracts, handbooks, policies and procedures in place. One day a very loyal, but junior, member of staff went off sick which was totally out of character. The period of sickness got extended and finally she revealed that she was diagnosed with cancer and was not likely to return to work any time soon due to the various treatments that were to follow.

Her contractual sick-pay period expired. Out of compassion, the MD continued her full pay for another six months. When the MD reduced it to half pay all hell broke loose. She and her family accused the MD of adding stress to their situation and generally being inconsiderate. The employer continued to pay half pay for about another year, until she rather sadly died. They then made a generous payment aimed at helping with the funeral costs.

These facts were not made public but the employee had discussed her arguments around her sickness pay dropping to half pay with colleagues. The family's astonishment at the generous final payment also got out.

It had been painful, but the MD felt they had done their best by their loyal employee by going well past any legal obligations, which helped with their own grieving process.

The next bit is, well, breath-taking.

A less loyal employee now goes off sick. The sickness gets extended and diagnosed as depression. The employee does not return to work and their sick pay period expires. In order to not add to the employee's stress the MD agrees to pay them for a defined period of 3 months on an ex gratia

> basis. The employee's expectation was that they would pay her indefinitely as they had with the previous long-term sick case. She raised a formal grievance – yes, honestly – and caused a great fuss.
>
> At this point the MD is the victim of her own generosity. By being inconsistent, albeit with good motives, she found herself in a maelstrom of HR and employment law problems.

So, the lesson is to be very careful about expectations!

The harsh reality is that generosity can create an expectation. A difficult, but key, learning is the value of treating everyone in exactly the same way regardless of your personal feelings towards them or their record of behaviour and loyalty. Additionally, having life insurance and/or critical illness insurance for staff may help you avoid the temptation to 'do the right' but inconsistent thing.

This is not to say that a rigid policy has to apply. Employers can still exercise 'management discretion' but the key, as always, is to set out the decision-making process in a clear and consistent way. So, for example, create a short list of criteria (say 3-5 points) that will be considered in the event that the company wants to exercise management discretion to pay an employee who is off sick. Include measurable and fair criteria such as:

- Length of service
- Record of previous attendance, excluding any long-term sickness or absence due to disability
- Conduct at work including attitude to job and colleagues (measurable via appraisals, performance records etc)
- Current disciplinary record

Having arrived at a list of criteria, implement a simple process so every case will be given the same consideration. So, for example, all instances where management discretion will be applied must be put before the directors of the company at a board meeting. Here, the case will be discussed, the criteria applied and a decision will be reached by the directors and recorded in the board minutes. The outcome will not necessarily be the same in each instance, but the process of consideration will be and, most importantly, the application of the process will be recorded and available when decisions are questioned or disputed.

```
Don't expect employees to value the same things as you

An entrepreneur we know had started a business and, after a
    few years, was keen to reward his senior employees. He
    also wanted to involve them in the business. Advised by
    his accountants he created an EMI scheme, a tax efficient
    share option programme. It gave each of his four senior
    people a stake in the business, free of charge.

When he told them this he had four different reactions:
One said, 'Wow, that's great, thanks.'
One said, 'Is that all I am getting?'
One said, 'I don't care about capital gain. I just want a
    bigger salary.'
One said, 'If you don't pay for my degree course I'm leaving.'

Just to make matters worse he had already paid £10,000 in fees
    to create the scheme. Two years later, only the first
    employee was still there.
```

Playing fairly is sometimes about understanding the differing expectations, priorities and perspectives of your employees. It is empathising with their idea of 'fair'. Treat them as they want to be treated not as you would want to be treated!

Do remember who's the boss

It is very easy to think that with all this red tape and employee rights that the tail is wagging the dog and, as a manager, you dare not do anything that might upset staff.

Well, here's some good news. You are still the *BOSS*. You can pretty much do what you want, when you want. Employment law and HR departments should not stop you doing what needs to be done. Their involvement is all about the *how* not the *what*.

Provided you are doing the right thing, for the right reasons, you can carry on. But, obviously, if your motives are dubious, or you are not behaving consistently or fairly, then you must move into the controlled zone where HR and employment law may need to guide your actions.

Here are some of the things that are still possible to do, fairly, and within the law:

- Dismissing people
- Changing terms and conditions
- Hiring people to a very tight specification
- Telling people clearly when they make a mistake
- Having people only when you need them
- Setting standards such as appearance, dress, how to deal with people and general behaviour

Removing under-performers from a business is entirely possible. There are multiple legal routes. The quickest and often least stressful, but not the cheapest, is a settlement agreement. The slowest and most involved is to take them through a performance review, highlight their under-performance areas, and give them time to improve. Depending on the circumstances, a more direct disciplinary route might be more appropriate. However, it is risky, illegal and generally not a good idea to use redundancy as the method to lose under-performers. We will cover this in more detail later.

Terms and conditions of employment often need to change to reflect a new business situation. An employment contract is a mutual agreement and, if both parties agree, they can change this readily with no fuss. However, you can enforce change yourself if one of three grounds exist; economic, technical or organisational. Cutting through the highfallutin' terminology, this means that if you have financial pressures, the way of working changes or the structure of your business is altered, you can legitimately change terms and conditions. The measure will obviously be the truth of the matter. If you connive a situational change just to change pay you are likely to get into difficulty. But, if it's obvious to everybody what's happening to the business, that should be enough to change the employment contract.

If you need a person with very specific skills or attributes you can select candidates accordingly. It's not discrimination to say you need somebody who speaks Italian because you do a lot of business in Italian. It's not discrimination to say you need somebody who can stay away from home a lot if there is a real business reason. It's not discrimination to say you need somebody with excellent local knowledge - a taxi driver, for example. If there's a genuine business reason you can hire to that need.

Speaking to people firmly is also perfectly legal. Browbeating them, swearing uncontrollably, manhandling them, singling people out or humiliating them is not. But, if you do not correct under-performance or bad behaviour it will continue. Why wouldn't it?

There are a number of 'flexible working' contract formats that allow employers and employees to find a situation that suits them both. Zero-hours contracts are an extreme version of this, which must be handled cautiously as we discussed earlier in the book. However, annualised hours are a perfectly neat way to vary working hours, with demand, over a year. Obviously, flexitime around a core minimum hours per day has been around for a long time. Sometimes job sharing is the right answer. The old-fashioned 'job and knock' system can be highly motivational in some situations, where you pay for a given task regardless of the time taken. As you can see, the employer can have a highly variable workforce if they want it as long as they play fair.

All organisations have a culture of their own. Whether it is created consciously and with purpose or it just happens organically is irrelevant. There is always a 'way things get done around here'. Employers can reasonably ask and expect their people to maintain and adhere to those standards. These things can manifest in a million different ways. It might be the dress code (you can generally insist on one), how to answer the phone, dealing with customers, how meetings are held, the language people use (is swearing allowed?), timekeeping, email style, cleanliness of the work space and so on. Provided everybody has the same standards to uphold and they are generally reasonable (insisting on Armani suits might not be!) then go for it.

```
Be clear about your 'why'. Is it fair and proportionate?

We have a client who moves in the high fashion and design
    world. In essence it sells style. The managing director is
    extremely sensitive to the way clients and the outside
    world perceive them. Image, darling, is everything.

If you had any kind of outward facing role the following would
    apply. None of this is optional.
  - You will be personally tutored by the MD or sales director
    in your sartorial choices. You must have the right
    wardrobe including jewellery, watches, glasses and so on.
     Your style is monitored and, where necessary, managed.
     You will keep updating it
  - Women must adhere to make-up standards and men need to be
    well groomed, especially when it comes to facial hair
```

DO

- You will not smoke at work or smell of smoke
- Personal hygiene must be well managed i.e. no body odour and perfume or aftershave must be used judiciously
- You will answer phone calls in three rings, emails in two hours and texts in one hour

These standards are high, sometimes subjective and very strictly enforced. However, the reasoning is proportionate to the requirements of the business and applied fairly and consistently across employees.

Like it or lump it, everybody knows the rules. It is not ambiguous or negotiable. The purpose of this 'cultural dynamic' forms an integral part of how the business sees itself and how others value the brand and how it operates. It is living the service it provides, it is part of its identity and is key to its success in attracting and retaining both customers and staff.

EMPLOYMENT LAW IS NOT FOR THE CONVENIENCE OF EMPLOYERS

Culture is 'the way we do things around here'

This client had a very singular vision and there was no room for non-compliance. The extreme nature of this vision was bordering on the compulsive and was definitely comical to the outside world.

To protect the brand we are going to lie about the product type. Let's say it's rolling pins and the company is Kitchco. Everybody, absolutely everybody, had to answer the phone like this: 'Hello, Kitchco. The best rolling pin in the world. How can I help you?'

You can understand why external calls would benefit from this but ALL internal calls had to be answered like this too. Which meant, if you called reception you got it once, when transferred you got it twice or three times! If you visited them all you could hear was the endless repetition of that phrase.

Whether you consider this to be brainwashing, over the top or just down right 'odd' it definitely had an impact.

Be under no illusion, their people believed they had 'the best rolling pin in the world'. That confidence comes out in everything they write, say or do. That must be a factor in the exceptional success of the business. It is now the brand leader in its field and was sold for a very large amount of money.

Do listen and watch

Back in the day the 'modern' management style advocated by all the gurus was MBWA – aka Management By Wandering Around. Although it has been around for decades, the term was coined by American management consultants Tom Peters and Robert H. Waterman in their 1982 book, *In Search of Excellence.* This ground-breaking insight into managing people was based on knowing what is going on in the office. What would we do without these people, eh?

Whilst it might seem obvious that this is a good idea, in our modern world, it's not as easy or straightforward as it might have once been. Take a situation where people work remotely, connected only by the digital world. Or, perhaps, where there are multiple sites across continents with many miles, time zones and local languages between them. There are also generational differences. A middle-aged senior executive may not have a clue what two 18-year olds are actually talking about, especially when every third word is 'like'. You might not even hear it because it's a text, WhatsApp or Instagram message.

There's a tendency to think 'it's all too difficult. Let's not bother.' Sitting in your cocooned office and not engaging with people is just so much simpler. Mmmm, your instincts tell you that's not smart.

What's the answer then? Well, in our experience there is no one 'answer'. Management, good management at least, is a combination of lots of things. But, most of it is common sense, hard work, intuition and doing the right things.

There is a whole 21st century tool kit available for MBWA in our new world. Some are formal while others are just being human.

Formal examples can include regular staff surveys, 360-degree feedback programmes, job swaps, suggestion schemes, staff committees, psychometric profiling, team building events, job evaluation schemes, measuring staff absence trends and exit interviews. Trying to win Sunday Times Top 100 employer status or a Platinum Investors In People ranking can help close the gap of understanding between management and their teams. These will give you an insight to what people in your business really think, what they might want and how they feel about the organisation and their relationship with it in the same way that MBWA does. As you might expect, if you use these initiatives you need to act on the outcomes as well as being seen to act on them.

Sometimes the outcomes from these initiatives are really challenging. A job evaluation scheme may force difficult pay changes. A 360-feedback programme might be a very hurtful look in the mirror. Being scored poorly in a Sunday Times Top 100 assessment is embarrassing. But if you don't want the answer, don't ask the question. If you do want the answer, then do something positive with it when it arrives. The following example gives you an insight in to what can happen if these tenets are ignored.

```
Don't raise expectations that you cannot meet

This organisation had been through a very rough period where
    survival was the order of the day. It was a global brand
    whose market had evaporated due to the rapid march of
    technology. They had barely survived, and in many ways
    were the 'last man standing' in their sector. Sales
    decline had stopped. The market had bottomed out and was
    now stable and, whilst a fraction of what it once was,
    there was a future to be had.

Unfortunately, the 'realignment' to the market – which, in
    real terms, meant downsizing and redundancies – had left
    the organisation in a terribly weakened state.
    Understandably, morale was low. Management at all levels
    was battle weary. There was no coherent, credible view of
    the future or a suitable business plan for the next steps.
    Everybody was fearful and there was no momentum. They had
    lost their sense of purpose.

To make matters worse, the work force in the factory that made
    the product was aging. Over 70% were likely to be
    considering retirement inside five years. This was a
    highly technical and well-skilled bunch of people.
```

Training new people in this industry takes years and they need a high level of engineering education before they start.

Some bright spark thought it would be helpful to get a sense of how the workforce was feeling. A staff survey was issued and the company promised to share feedback with the employees.

Unsurprisingly, some of the results were critical of management. Employees begged for effective leadership and sought reassurance about their future with concerns about pay. For the senior team this was all too much.

The results lead to paralysis. What should they do? What should they say? The financial position was extremely constraining. They could not 'buy' their way out of this situation or make promises to change things under current circumstances.

There then followed a lengthy pause in which they did not talk with the work force.

The outcome, quite predictably, was a further disgruntlement amongst their people and even greater disalignment amongst the senior team on how to take the business forward. A positive engagement had produced a seriously negative outcome because they hadn't considered the consequences of the survey and whether they were able to make changes in response.

> HANDS UP WHO THINKS I'M DOING A GREAT JOB?

The moral of the story is to only take these steps if you want answers and intend to deal with them constructively. Asking the question always raises expectations that there will be an answer and improvement. Raising expectations that cannot be met is always worse than not raising them at all. But this does not mean taking no action.

```
Help your managers to see themselves as others see them

A client received a 360-degree feedback report and made the
    following comments. 'I have triangulated this. I have
    spoken to my mum, my wife and my friends. The feedback's
    right. I am an a***hole'.

This was a very senior man in an organisation with a large
```

number of staff. His interpersonal skills were non-existent. He was intelligent, witty, insightful, brave and brutally unpleasant to work with.

He set about genuinely trying to improve his engagement. It was successful to a degree. He did manage to invest time in social interaction. He learned to say please, thank you and well done to colleagues. In a marginal sense, he became more approachable. He was markedly more 'user friendly'. People commented on it. However, under pressure or seeing results and outputs threatened, he would lose some of these advantages. Sadly, he was hard-wired to be insensitive but at least his increased self-awareness meant he was getting better results from people most of the time and the number of 'incidents' reduced.

Simply put, he will always be in the risk zone, legally, but hopefully that risk is reduced and people enjoy working with him just a little bit more.

Summary

The informal ways to do MBWA are obvious. Talk to people. Listen to what they have to say. In meetings and conferences, look at body language. Read people. When things like grievances arise look for the underlying issue, as there usually is one, rather than focusing on the process or 'defending' the corporate position. Seek input from people and use it. Empower junior supervisors to watch and listen so there is a culture of trust and sharing of concerns.

If you are losing good people at a high rate talk to them, informally, and find out why.

Arrange opportunities to engage with people at all levels and talk with them in ways they understand. With remote workforces find ways to contact them, such as webinars, conference calls, video conferences, Skype and so on. Emails and message boards will help but one-to-one contact is invaluable. Also, be aware that a lot of chatter goes on via social media and this kind of interaction can be informative for a manager. However, try not to stalk people and assess feedback in balance to the wider group of employees. It might only be people with strong views or agendas that are evident in this sphere so don't assume it's a representative sample.

The best way to deal with employment issues is, of course, to not have them in the first place. That often comes from low-level interventions to fix things before they become issues. Listening to, watching and engaging with your people are big steps towards defusing potentially difficult situations or not allowing them to arise at all.

Remember

A lot of employment law is not always intuitive. Here, we will cover five key situations and topics where it would be really helpful to keep your wits about you:
   - Remember: TUPE is tricky
   - Remember: redundancy is about roles not people
   - Remember: employees have responsibilities too
   - Remember: employment law has a few very sensitive areas
   - Remember: people management is constantly evolving

Remember: TUPE is tricky

TUPE regulations are the absolute epitome of the law of unintended consequences. What is a genuinely well-intentioned piece of legislation can produce precisely the wrong outcome. It can also drag in other, unrelated, employment laws.

TUPE (Transfer of Undertakings and Protection of Employment) was initially introduced into UK law in 1981. It endeavours to protect employee rights when ownership of an organisation changes. It was born out of some really bad behaviour by employers in days gone by. For example, dinner ladies employed by the local authority on Friday may be employed by an outsourced contract caterer on Monday but on much reduced terms. Same job, same place, but less pay. Not a very nice way to treat people.

Simplistically, the legal entity of the employer is less relevant than the actual job circumstances. If the role is effectively the same, either side of the ownership transfer, then TUPE will apply. Thus, you cannot hide behind a different company as the new employer and impose new conditions on employees.

That is it in essence, but the circumstances often change, for good reason, and the correct application of TUPE can become very unclear. For example, geography can be a key consideration. If the location the jobs will operate at changes significantly then TUPE may not apply. Be aware that in that case redundancy might be triggered so be careful about who picks that responsibility up. Our advice is, if in doubt on TUPE, and there is usually good reason to be doubtful, get experienced professional advice.

Here are a couple of examples of how TUPE can cause problems for you as a manager.

Unintended consequence number one. A company goes into administration. If the company or its trade are not bought by another business all jobs will be lost. But, if it is bought by another company there may have to be changes to salaries and numbers of employees in order to make it a feasible business again. However, if it is bought then TUPE applies so the employees' employment rights are protected – so no changes to T's & C's or staff numbers (without redundancy costs). So, many businesses in administration fail to rise like phoenixes out of the ashes because of TUPE. Consequently, far from protecting employment it actually threatens jobs. Of course, there are charlatans out there capable of putting sound businesses into administration to reset their employment contracts. Hopefully that is a very small minority.

Unintended consequence number two. This is fascinating and shocking. TUPE says terms and conditions for employees must stay the same after a transfer. Seems simple.

Equality regulations say employers cannot pay two different rates of pay for the same job within their company. Also simple.

Different employers can and do pay someone doing the same job differently, of course.

There's the problem.

```
Consequences of TUPE

Cleaning company Sparkling Ltd. buys another cleaning company;
    Dusters Ltd.

Dusters is barely profitable and needs to be part of a bigger
    organisation like Sparkling to survive. Dusters pays the
    minimum wage and not much else. Sparkling pays well over
    the minimum wage and provides benefits in kind.

Once Dusters is owned by Sparkling there's a need to bring the
    terms and conditions in line. Sparkling employees won't
    accept a pay cut so guess what happens? Duster's employees
    get a pay rise and the company's financial position is
```

```
    put in jeopardy.

  It's sometimes called 'harmonisation' but it doesn't always
    lead to much harmony!
```

Now, this was a very simple example. But what if the there are multiple layers of differences in terms and conditions between the two organisations? One has higher basic pay but the other pays good bonuses. What if one pays lower pension contributions but has medical insurance? What if the management structures are different so a like-for-like comparison is hard? It can be a mess, and extremely expensive, as the tendency is to levitate to the higher terms. It could negate the viability of the transfer entirely, potentially threatening jobs, rather than protecting them.

Also, this example belies some complexity in the legal position, because employees are strongly protected against harmonisation.

The rule is that terms and conditions must not be varied by the outgoing or incoming employer if the principal reason for the variation is the transfer. Rights given by statute are more important than any contractual agreements, so even if variations are agreed by the employee, the changes will still be legally ineffective.

One of the most common questions we are asked by employers, who are contemplating or have recently completed a TUPE transfer, is how they might 'safely' harmonise terms and conditions.

Unfortunately, we have to start by highlighting that harmonisation is prohibited by TUPE and is always unlawful unless it falls within one of these categories:

- Where the reason for variation is completely unrelated to the transfer
- Where the variation is favourable to the employee
- Where there is an economic, technical or organisational reason (ETO reason) entailing changes in the workforce and the employer and employee agree on the variation
- When the terms of the employment contract permit variation, for example a mobility clause
- Some insolvency situations
- A change to the place of employment after the transfer can be an ETO reason
- If there has been a collective agreement, that incorporates terms and conditions, those may be varied after more than a year from the transfer, as long as the employee's terms are no less favourable overall than they were before the variation

Yes, this is completely mad! As we said TUPE is tricky.

```
Harmonisation in a large enterprise

We have some insight into events at a local Higher Education
    College.

The college merged with another local college in 2017. Whilst
    general terms and conditions were broadly similar there
    were a number of differences and inevitable anomalies. So,
    holidays, sick pay, expense allowances, notice and role
    categorisations had differences.

This is in an environment where the reason for merger was to
    save money and the staff had strong but cooperative union
```

representation. So, over 2 years, 1 massive Job Evaluation scheme, and hours of representative negotiation and staff consultation later, they have finally got to a formal proposal of the harmonisation changes.

At the time of writing that proposal had not been accepted, and probably would not be put to bed for several more months. So about 3 years and lots of disruption, distraction, unsettled staff and costs to 'harmonise' 2 relatively simple teams.

Now, interestingly for an employer TUPE can provide some upside. Don't get too excited because there is an element of sting in the tail that our next example will show.

As an employer if you have a need to reorganise your corporate structure (e.g. put businesses into different entities) or you sell the business, staff do not get to choose whether TUPE applies. They simply get transferred across if the TUPE criteria are met.

That sting in the tail:

Complexity and distraction

Our client, a large, growing professional services firm got to a point where it wanted to put different client service streams into separate legal entities, albeit within the same group and with no impact on employee rights or length of service. In practical terms it was an administrative rather than commercial initiative.

EMPLOYMENT LAW IS NOT FOR THE CONVENIENCE OF EMPLOYERS

```
There arose a very clear obligation to consult with all staff
    and take on board any concerns and recommendations. Indeed
     it created the need to get detailed advice from lawyers
     to ensure no further implications arose. Obviously staff
     get nervous when things like this happen and potentially
     read all sorts into an otherwise innocent situation.

Amazing how something small and apparently straightforward can
    become a much bigger, more complex thing, with all the
     distraction that creates.
```

Summary

The overall learnings regarding TUPE are:

- Take professional advice early and prior to the commencement of commercial negotiations
- The devil is in the detail. Make sure you assign a team to ensure that you have everything you need to comply with the legislation (whether you are an incoming or outgoing employer)
- Find out the real 'on the ground' information about the other party and don't just rely on desk research or financial data
- There is no end date but, time and distance from the date of transfer can help achieve changes however complex or far-reaching
- Beware of unintended consequences such as harmonisation and the need for complex staff consultation
- If TUPE does not apply and the transfer goes ahead staff may well be redundant. How does that impact commercial negotiations and which party has the legal responsibility (and the bill!).

Remember: redundancy is about roles not people

Redundancy is a potentially fair reason for dismissing an employee. However, an employment tribunal will not treat a dismissal as a redundancy dismissal unless it is caused by:

- the closure of a business
- the closure of a particular workplace
- a diminished need for employees to carry out work of a particular kind

So, a 'true' redundancy is a potentially legally-compliant way to reduce a workforce. With that in mind, the law does not allow this to be a shortcut to "getting rid of people" you don't want in the company. It is not a euphemism for sweeping away under-performers or people who 'don't fit in'.

Not only is that illegal, but not following the formal redundancy process, very carefully, can expose the employer to some extremely strict penalties.

We have seen many employers play fast and loose with redundancy. So, to expose the risks here is a brief outline of a legally acceptable process.

The First opportunity to get it right. Planning.

Before commencing redundancy procedures, management should ensure that one of the earlier situations demonstrably applies.

Redundancy will normally be accepted as a "fair" reason for dismissal as long as:

- the redundancy is genuine
- the organisation's procedures have been followed and employees have been treated reasonably
- affected employees have been consulted (big issue – check below)
- objective criteria to select who will be made redundant have been agreed and applied fairly and consistently
- managers have looked for suitable alternative work for those whose jobs are at risk but have established that there is nothing else available

As you can see, at no time does it mention under-performance as a result of incompetence, attitude, attendance, disciplinary record or anything relating to the quality of the employee. This is why using redundancy to get rid of people you don't want is therefore a perilous endeavour.

Genuine redundancy relates to *removal of roles* or *numbers in a role* it is not about individuals at this point.

The second opportunity to get it right. Consult

As soon as management have worked out that they are *considering* (yes, that does mean thinking about) a redundancy programme, they are required to consult with those staff who are *potentially* affected. This obligation means that the decision about who will be made redundant must not have already been made. It's a schoolboy error to announce to staff the outcome of a redundancy programme prior to consultation.

Now please make a note that if the numbers are more than 20 this can be a really drawn out affair – absolutely not a quick fix.

Where the proposal is to make 20 or more employees redundant, there is a statutory duty to consult either the trade unions or, if there are none, elected employee representatives. This is known as collective consultation and is in addition to individual consultation.

Collective consultation must begin "in good time":

- Where 100 or more employees are to be made redundant, consultation must take place at least 45 days before notice of the first dismissal is issued
- Where 20 or more employees are to be made redundant, consultation must take place at least 30 days before notice of the first dismissal is issued

If there will be fewer than 20 employees the individuals who are affected should be consulted on an individual basis. This should start at least 14 days before notice of the first dismissal issued.

Once again not a quick fix.

To make your administration department deliriously happy, the icing on the cake is that if you anticipate that you will need to dismiss 20 or more employees from your business, you must notify the Secretary of State for Business, Energy and Industrial Strategy (BEIS), in writing, of the proposal and before giving notice to terminate any of the relevant employees' contracts.

Failure to consult with employees renders the employer liable to a criminal conviction and a fine. This is called a "protective award". **The protective award can be up to 90 days' actual pay for each employee and there is no cap.**

Best not get that bit wrong then.

Also, remember that the law's perspective is that there may be alternatives to the redundancy programme. So, before you roll it out, you need to have checked with the staff involved to see if they have any bright ideas. Aka *Consultation*

As set out at the start, this is not a shortcut to dismissal.

The third opportunity to get it right. Selection for Redundancy

The next step of this process is to select the individuals to be made redundant in a fair and transparent way. If all roles are going it's fairly straightforward but, if not, you need clear, fair and reasonable grounds to select candidates for redundancy. If you rig the criteria for selection in order to dismiss employees you want to get rid of there is a good chance that somebody will claim unfair selection for redundancy and this is a sure-fire invitation to the employment tribunal.

It may be that there are members of staff in more than one department doing similar jobs and, if so, your managers will need to consider whether those employees should be included in the 'pool' of those to be considered for redundancy.

This is where employees feel they are applying for their own job as they are assessed against the various criteria.

It's not allowed to select on absence because of pregnancy, or maternity leave, nor should absence from work for a reason linked to disability count. Personal factors should not be taken into account when making this decision. Marital status, number of children or other dependants, etc. are all irrelevant. Using age or age-related criteria would also likely be unlawful.

Each affected employee should be informed, at a meeting, of their assessment and how it was arrived at, and given an opportunity to challenge it. The employer should always be able to defend its decisions.

The employee is also entitled to their contractual notice, or statutory notice if this is longer.

Unless the circumstances are critical, therefore, redundancy should not be something which is rushed through. If the proper procedures are not followed, you run the risk that the redundancy dismissals will be unfair, with the potential for successful claims at the employment tribunal.

The fourth opportunity to get it right. Moving on

Don't forget about the 'survivors' who remain in your business. Everyone is affected when there are redundancies. Even after those made redundant have left, there will be an unsettled feeling for some time. Staff will be aware that there is always the potential for further job losses. Serious thought and effort should be made to help these people move forward.

So, even from this quick overview you can see that redundancy does not lend itself easily to getting rid of under-performers. So, the message is clear; don't do it!

Redundancy as a shortcut!

Our client had an underperforming accountant. Whilst they were unhappy with their performance, what they were doing was imperative to ongoing operations, so the client schemed to hire an assistant accountant and when they had completed their induction and training, proceeded to make the original accountant redundant.

Whilst the actual process for making the accountant redundant was conducted properly, it was self-evidently all contrived to avoid a difficult performance management situation. Needless to say the accountant cried foul and a settlement was ultimately agreed.

Whilst this was a means to an end, it was neither the most honest nor the cheapest route. Had the client consulted us earlier the outcome would have been somewhat different.

Summary

Don't enter the redundancy process with a closed mind, a predetermined outcome or a desire to use it to 'clean house'. A bone fide redundancy process is a legal way to terminate employees but remember the strict legal definition. It's really important to behave in a consistent and fair manner. Getting it wrong can be very pricey.

Remember: employees have responsibilities too

As we said earlier, an employment contract is a two-way agreement. In exchange for money, employees agree to perform an agreed set of tasks. They also agree to a lot of other things:

- To turn up on time
- To behave according to the organisation's rules, usually contained in a handbook
- To look after the legitimate interests of the business
- To be available for work
- To do the work to acceptable standards
- To obey a reasonable instruction
- To not behave recklessly or in an unsafe manner
- To not steal property, whether tangible or intellectual, or act in a fraudulent way

For more senior or sensitive roles there might even be specific rules around confidentiality, not poaching staff or customers, working for a competitor or stealing intellectual property.

In simple terms, if they do not keep their side of the contract you can take action including, ultimately, firing them. There is a process to follow but, in the end, the result can be a parting of ways.

If an employee doesn't fulfil their contractual obligations and you ask them to leave then a settlement agreement is often used to bring the relationship to a swift end. This is essentially a legally-binding agreement made between an employer and employee (or ex-employee) in which the employee agrees not to pursue claims in relation to their employment or its termination in return, generally, for a financial settlement.

However, although this protects the employer against unfair dismissal claims, employees can use what was said during pre-termination negotiations as evidence in other types of claims, for example a discrimination claim or a claim for breach of contract.

Also, it is important to remember that pre-termination discussions are not protected at all under the settlement agreement rules if the employee has been dismissed for an unfair reason, for example taking maternity leave or asserting the right to the national minimum wage. Also, the content of the discussions is protected only to the extent that the tribunal considers just. For example, if the employer's conduct during pre-termination negotiations amounts to bullying or intimidation, the tribunal can decide that the claimant can use this as evidence.

For the document to be legally binding there are a series of legal formalities that need to be complied with. The employee must have received independent legal advice from a relevant adviser as to the terms and effect of the agreement and, in particular, its effect on his or her ability to pursue rights before an employment tribunal. There must be in force, when the adviser gives the legal advice, a contract of insurance or professional indemnity insurance covering the risk of a claim by the employee in respect of loss arising as a result of the advice. It is highly likely that, if you have not taken professional advice in drawing up the document, you will find yourself in protracted negotiations on individual clauses or having to accept unwanted obligations if you want the agreement to be struck.

It is usual to make a contribution towards the employee's legal costs (at the time of writing the going rate is c.£250.00).

If in doubt, you should seek specific advice on the tax treatment of the various payments being made and include a tax indemnity from the employee in the agreement to make them liable for unpaid tax.

We simply have too many Settlement Agreement examples to single any out!

They vary from CEOs to administration clerks and factory floor employees. In recent times the confidentiality aspect, the NDA clause (non-disclosure agreement), is coming under increased scrutiny. Especially, where it is being used to gag whistle blowers – so be warned…

We see many different approaches to the relationship with staff. The owner of one business we know sees 60% staff turnover per year as a badge of honour. And, very recently a business owner was described to us as: 'A mill owner born 100 years too late'.

> R.S.I.? POPPYCOCK, GIRL! WHY, YOU'VE BARELY WORKED FIFTEEN HOURS TODAY!

Summary

Whilst employment law gives staff many protections, it doesn't override basic principles. The employer exchanges fair money for fair labour. Ultimately, it's a simple bargain.

Remember: employment law has a few very sensitive areas

Pregnancy and maternity is one of these highly sensitive areas. Most employers have a basic understanding of their obligations in relation to pregnant employees. However, according to a 2017 survey of employers by EHRC Research, 41% of employers say that pregnancy in the workplace puts "an unnecessary cost burden" on their businesses. According to this survey:

- 44% of employers believe that women who have had more than one pregnancy while in the same job can be a "burden" to their team
- 40% of employers claim to have seen at least one pregnant woman in their workplace 'take advantage' of their pregnancy
- 32% believe women who become pregnant and new mothers in work are "generally less interested in career progression" than other employees

These findings indicate that there are still a large number of employers who at best don't understand or worst don't respect employment law as it relates to pregnant women and new mothers. They may also reflect a simple reality that in very small businesses maternity presents real management challenges. Challenges that need to be met – fairly.

Pregnancy and maternity discrimination differ from other forms of direct discrimination because they do not require the complainant to show that she has been treated less favourably than someone else. Instead, she must show that she has been treated unfavourably because of her pregnancy or maternity leave.

For example, if an employee has high absence levels due to pregnancy-related sickness, it would be unlawful for an employer to take action, under its absence policy, as a result of this. There is no need for the employee to compare her treatment with that of someone who is not pregnant.

Many issues we see are connected with the refusal by the employer of part-time or job-share work for employees returning from maternity leave and these would be considered under the provisions relating to indirect sex discrimination.

Other sensitive areas include disability, age, gender pay gap, paternity and a growing one; the 'intern'.

Internships have been around what feels like forever. Depending on your perspective, or dare we say the facts of the matter, these are fabulous opportunities to gain invaluable experience or merciless exploitation of vulnerable people by extracting free labour. We have rules around the minimum wage and ultimately this area will be judged accordingly.

```
Internships on steroids!

  We have all probably read about large food outlets asking
    candidates to work full shifts unpaid as part of their
    selection and/or induction process. University students
    often do summer jobs to add experience to their studies
    which are sometimes unpaid.

  Well, a few years ago we met a business with offices around
```

the world that took 'free labour' to a whole new level. Well-heeled parents are charged (yes, charged tens of thousands) for organising internships for their offspring in high profile organisations globally. These network developing, CV enhancing, golden opportunities are so prized by a certain audience that the fees are seen as well worth the investment. Seeing is believing.

Summary

There's a sea-change occurring in the conduct of 'the modern workplace', what constitutes acceptable and unacceptable behaviour by employers has changed radically even from five years ago. Regardless of personal view points, there are, and will continue to be, increasingly sensitive areas.

Remember: people management is constantly evolving

As we said originally, employment law tries to adopt our wider values as a society, so that behaviour at work is in line with general behaviour. It is therefore regularly evolving, as societal norms and attitudes evolve.

As we write this book there are a few areas where we suspect the law will play catch up over the next few years. Therefore, it's likely that employers are going to find more regulation and constraints in areas that hitherto were either unregulated or had vague and indirect standards implied.

Concrete changes are obviously incredibly difficult to predict but here goes:

As a community we are becoming increasingly aware, and sincerely accepting, of the presence of mental illness. At one time 'suffering from stress' was seen as a sign of weakness and employers ignored their role in employee's mental wellbeing, feeling it was a problem that should be left at home. The truth is that many people spend at least 50% of their waking hours at work during the week. Also, we are so digitally connected that we're rarely truly unplugged from work, even at weekends or on holiday. Employers have some responsibility therefore. The question is, how much?

It seems to us that we can expect stricter and specific legislation protecting people with mental health issues in the work place. If an employee becomes mentally unwell the employer could be seen as responsible if they didn't take appropriate steps to mitigate those risks. It may end up looking very much like rules protecting pregnant women. This could well be extended into health and safety regulations too.

Regardless of Brexit, we believe we should expect a whole new set of rules controlling immigration. The reality will be that the government is going to get increasingly stuck between 'controlling our borders' and satisfying demand for people, both skilled and unskilled. The government has previously 'passed the buck' on this issue to employers, landlords and travel businesses so it may end up being increasingly your responsibility. We are not sure what it will consist of but expect more forms to fill in, rules around admission and right to stay, and lots of new penalties. Expect the rules to keep changing as the economy evolves and left or right-wing governments hold sway.

Social media and the digital world is continuing to change our lives, for good or ill. Regardless of the EU's General Data Protection Regulations (GDPR) it is pretty obvious that lawmakers are going to have get a tighter grip on this runaway train. One way would be to make employers vicariously liable for the behaviour of their staff. You read it here first.

Another area of change we see coming is the shifting of social responsibility for people from the government to employers. In the USA employers pick up the tab for medical cover for their staff. As our inability to fund social care becomes acute (no pun intended) expect responsibility for that provision to be increasingly shifted to employers. Again, the government have demonstrated that they're happy to move in this direction, just look at the Apprentice Levy. It might be that the government just wants employers to provide funding. It might be that employers have to accept responsibility for direct service provision (for example, in Scandinavia there are rules around providing canteens) or it might be some form of employment quota system to ensure there are jobs for an ageing population. Again, here the government have demonstrated their willingness to involve the employer in this stuff - just look at how they have reshaped the workplace pension where the administration and costs have been passed on to employers.

Another recent trend is the emerging management guru mantra that suggests 'engaged employees' are a good thing. People, clever people, are writing books, giving TED talks, running training courses and selling 'how to' consultancy on this. They really are.

Nobody can provide empirical evidence that happy staff = more productivity = more profit. Of course, there are lots of anecdotes, but no proof.

We have seen the most cynical and nasty exploitation of people along with the most sincere attempts to be a very nice boss. Unfortunately, some of the worst behaviour has produced excellent financial results.

Equally, we have seen how really bad management can create mayhem and destroy a business.

Employee engagement boils down to having people truly interested in the business. If they are excited, involved or committed to the cause they will undoubtedly contribute 'above and beyond'. That can only be a good thing for everybody. But it's not new.

In particular, organisations that are going through extreme change – a financial turnaround or exponential growth - really benefit from engaged employees. This is often more straightforward to create because there is an obvious upside for employees to supporting the inherent change involved.

For most employers, employee engagement is likely to morph into a more generic 'listen to what they say' and 'behave sensibly' strategy. Our prediction is that the employee engagement phenomenon will be scaled back to an acknowledgement that those good old-fashioned values of trust, fairness, honesty and openness will continue to go a long way in promoting a happy and productive work environment.

Related to engagement is a renewed focus on social and emotional well-being. Far from connecting people, research has found that technology is actually making employees feel more disconnected than ever before. The increasing use of apps, text and social media to communicate rather than calling or actually walking around to speak to people face-to-face is causing 46% of adult workers to report feeling lonely with only 53% saying they have meaningful, in-person social interactions on a daily basis.

When employees don't feel connected to their colleagues or the organisation they are likely to demonstrate much lower levels of engagement or simply leave the organisation.

We wrote earlier about the incidence of stress, anxiety and depression in the workplace today and this research supports the view that employees are increasingly reporting feeling stressed and don't feel their organisations really prioritise their social and emotional wellbeing.

So, what can you do?

Science shows that positive peak experiences stand out and overshadow negative experiences at work. So, focus your attention on 'peak experiences' that build those connections. For example, build a workplace culture that makes face-to-face connection between colleagues a priority. Go and talk to each other rather than just emailing or texting. Promote employee wellbeing, for example, by creating a culture that does not stigmatize mental ill health but promotes understanding via training and education.

Develop active social strategies that bring colleagues together and perhaps try to link this to worthwhile activities that give back to the local community.

Celebrate successes (whether individual or team-based), recognise and promote careers and career development, select and educate managers who are recognised by their peers and reports as leaders. Work diligently and consistently on your daily communications so that these unite and bond your work colleagues to each other and the organisation rather than causing division.

Finally, much has been written about the new generations and how employers need to modify their management style to accommodate them.

Well, guess what, every new generation is different to their predecessors. For good or ill. We can't see this changing, so stop making excuses and work to understand what they want from an employer and do your best to put it in place. The low-risk strategy might be just to have a chat with them but, remember, you are living in their world they are not living in yours!

Epilogue

As we said at the beginning, we are author virgins who have tried to distill our personal experiences of 40 years into a few pithy examples and anecdotes that may serve as examples of how, or indeed warnings about how not, to manage people.

It strikes us that there are a few principles that might serve us, as managers and employers, well as we face into our futures.

Ensure that all of your managers are involved in as many methods of proper people management as possible. Train them, particularly if they swerve 'difficult conversations' with their staff. Incentivise them so that they understand the importance of continuous feedback (particularly with Millennial and Gen Z staff) and reward them for effective outcomes.

Focus, wherever possible, on the positive. Celebrate success, identify opportunities for growth and make this growth creative not just based on promotion. Work to identify how your employees' job aligns with their personal sense of purpose and your purpose as an organisation. Mentor and coach your employees and empower them with response-ability. This is not a typo but relates to the ability to respond to any work situation more effectively by increasing their self-awareness.

Most of all, work on providing "peak employee experiences" for your employees, in the same way that you strive to provide this for your customers or clients.

Employment law can be an ass. Employment law can be a pain. But, you know what, we are a better society for it than without it. I am not sure we really look back on the Victorian industrialists without thinking – how did they get away with that?

Now, one last anecdote to prove that there are loopholes left, and hopefully put a smile on your face. A true story. Honest.

We have a client who recruits people based on star sign. Yep – 'get me a Taurus' she is oft heard to say. At the point of writing there is no law against being a zodiacist.

Funny old world.

Graham and Jane *(as an equal opportunities employer it was my turn to go first – Graham)*